D1601699

★ 1,001 THINGS ★

REPUBLICANS

GET RIGHT

A COMPLETE GUIDE
—— FOR VOTERS ——

BILL O'RIGHTS

CASTLE POINT BOOKS
NEW YORK

www.stmartins.com
www.castlepointbooks.com

The Castle Point Books trademark is owned by Castle Point Publishing, LLC.
Castle Point books are published and distributed by St. Martin's Press.

ISBN 978-1-250-25667-6 (trade paperback)

Our books may be purchased in bulk for promotional, educational, or business use.
Please contact your local bookseller or the Macmillan Corporate and Premium
Sales Department at 1-800-221-7945, extension 5442, or by email
at MacmillanSpecialMarkets@macmillan.com.

First Edition: October 2019

10 9 8 7 6 5 4 3 2 1

⋆ CONTENTS ⋆

★ 1 ★

OUR FAMILY VALUES

OUR FAMILY VALUES

OUR FAMILY VALUES

OUR FAMILY VALUES

OUR FAMILY VALUES

★ 2 ★

WINNING ECONOMIC POLICIES

WINNING ECONOMIC POLICIES

★ **3** ★

OUR PLAN TO HELP

THE WORKING

CLASS

OUR PLAN TO HELP THE WORKING CLASS

★ 4 ★

REPUBLICAN DIVERSITY INITIATIVES

★ 5 ★

CLIMATE CHANGE STRATEGY

★ 6 ★

OUR BALANCED BUDGET PLANS

★ 7 ★

HOW TO WIN WITH TARIFFS

REASONS TO KEEP THE ELECTORAL COLLEGE

★9★

OUR HEALTH CARE PLAN

★ 10 ★

IMMIGRANTS WE LOVE

BIBLIOGRAPHY

BIBLIOGRAPHY

INDEX